Let's

D.I.G.

The Official Workbook for

The

M.A.P.

Chester L. Hall Jr, M.Ed, CLC, CALC
A GOODLIFE!! Coaching Publication

Chester L. Hall Jr, M.Ed, CLC, CALC
    Let's D.I.G. (Deep Insightful Growth) - The M.A.P. Workbook
    52 pp.
    ISBN-13: **978-0692721667**
    ISBN-10: **0692721665**

1. Self-Help   2. Personal Development
3. Life Coaching
I. Title

Copyediting by Nyoka Hall
Page Layout & Design by Chester Hall
Cover Design by Chester Hall

Introduction:

Hey! I hope you had the opportunity to read The M.A.P. and incorporate it into your life. If you have...WELCOME BACK! If you haven't read it...WELCOME! For those that don't know, in November of 2015, I published a personal development book based off my experiences and encounters with students, clients, teachers, parents, and the general public called The Massive Action Plan or M.A.P. It was founded in my years as a school board administrator, teacher, counselor, and student of self-help books. Although it was a short, but awesome read, it eventually became my coaching plan for young adults and adults alike. If you haven't read it, might I recommend you pick it up.

So, why am I writing The M.A.P. - Let's D.I.G? Well, for a few reasons. The first being if anyone else is like me, no matter what the book tells you to do in the text or margins, you just refuse to write, tab, highlight, fill-in-the-blank, or otherwise make the pages look like they were just butchered by a 9th grade English teacher. It just messes up the integrity of the script. Also, there's never enough room to take decent notes anyway. So what does one do? You either buy a second copy of the book (which isn't bad either!) to do all of your note taking, or you keep a separate notebook to keep all of your goodies in. This leads me to my next point...

My readers needed something to write in! Whenever I asked readers, or clients, to work on an exercise, they were scurrying to grab sheets of paper, a binder, spiral notebook, composition book, or whatever to log their writing and activities in. I even told readers to do this on page 32! #ImSoSorry! The other side of the story was that they didn't even bother writing anything if it wasn't right there for them to do so. This was happening during sessions...I could only imagine what was happening to those who weren't working directly with me! That kind of defeats the point of logging your activities if it doesn't stick with the book. I've seen copies of The M.A.P. with folded papers inside of them, copies mixed in with notebooks for their kids' assignments, or what I call "here-there" notes...some of it's over here, some of it's over there. I'm ecstatic that people think enough of it to work the exercises, but that's not productive...is it? I didn't think so. Although this will be categorized as a workbook with plenty of space to work and hash out ideas, it will still have some extra "nuggets" not in the book. Plus, it just looks freaking awesome to have a matching workbook dedicated to your success! #VainMuch? Yep! Next point...

Those Golden Nuggets, and I'm not talking about the preformed, deep fried, chicken slurry bites either! These are those points of interest that have been given to me by readers, clients, and my own musings. I felt it was important to include them to help the thought process along. I have met readers that have reported back to me requesting assistance in getting on the right track. I explain to them that regardless of what I say or the guidance I give it is completely up to them how the book is interpreted. This usually results in me still helping to jog their brains, which ultimately gets them moving. I wanted to create more guidance in the book, while giving space to muse, and not rewriting the book as a whole. From here on out, I will be calling those nuggets "Coins." (Fits the theme better!) So be on the lookout for them! And the last point...

D.I.G. stands for "Deep Insightful Growth." I want your journey through The M.A.P. to be all encompassing. If there was something you didn't get a chance to explore in depth just by reading the book, this should allow you to really probe you mind, spirit, and soul, therefore creating a solid foundation for serious growth. So, if you've already read The M.A.P., great for you! Take this workbook and get crackin'! If you haven't read the book, well, take a bit more time and do so while working through this manual. It will probably make more sense to you this way anyway. Are you ready? Well alright then! LET'S D.I.G!

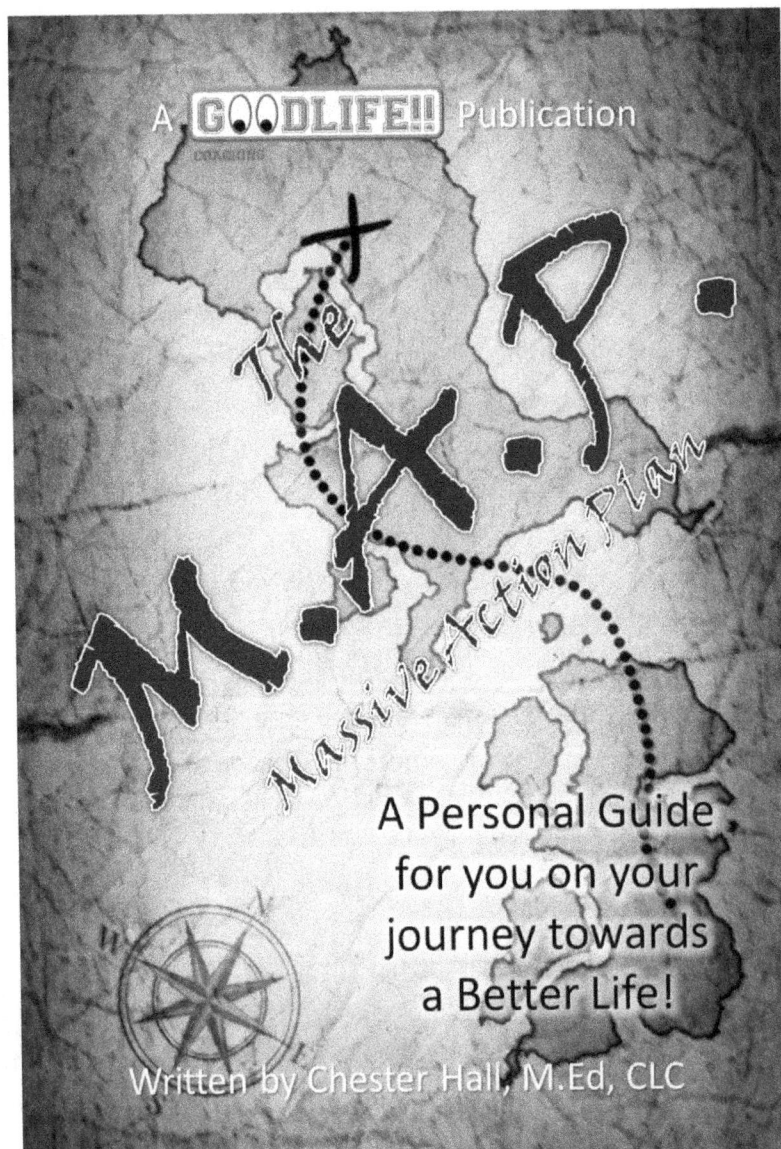

A GOODLIFE!! Publication

The M.A.P.

Massive Action Plan

A Personal Guide for you on your journey towards a Better Life!

Written by Chester Hall, M.Ed, CLC

Before We Begin...

I have to get this out there because it is a standard exercise in any coaching practice, and I didn't put it in the book. Silly me! But, it is a fundamental tool coaching tool. It's called the Wheel of Life. Not exactly the catchiest of names, but it illustrates its purpose. The Wheel of Life is used as a snapshot of your current state in life. It allows you to see exactly where you need to focus your time and energy, thus creating a positive flow of activity into all areas from those few. Most wheels have between seven and ten sections that cover everything from work life to spirituality, and it creates this image based on personal ratings of you from zero, serving as non-existent or very bad, to ten, representing daily practice and complete fulfillment. I enjoy sharing this with clients, and it really hits home when they lay it all out there on paper. I have some stories where people have literally broken down into tears and poured their souls out to me after visualizing their wheel. So although it may seem like a simple exercise, it is a powerful one! The ultimate wheel is one that could "roll" on its own without you feeling any bumps on the road, or stops itself dead in its tracks. We in the coaching profession call that the "Golden Circle," and it should be what everyone strives for in their lives...all nines and/or tens!

On the next page I have placed a typical W.O.L. You will see this exact same wheel two more times over the completion of this manual. I want you to fill this one out, honestly, and the rest of them as you encounter them through the text. After filling out the first, identify at least two to three areas that stand out to you which could use some improvement, but identify one that you are high in. Using that high point, try to find ways to incorporate the low points into your high one. Consider this, that one bright spot is the area where you have activities that you enjoy doing and probably work in regularly. When you begin to blend that area together with the others, your "needs improvement" areas will not feel like they need improving so much, and they will gradually rise to a higher level. Need an example? Okay...what if your spiritual life was a solid, unwavering ten, but your personal development/education section was lacking. A way to bring that area up may be asking the pastor to implement a night school program in the church, where participants could learn new skills. Because you love your church family, and you enjoy being there, you'd probably find yourself spending more time at the church learning than just on Sunday morning, and you'd be more prone to attend classes regularly. Here's another...maybe your financial sector is low, but your environmental area is high, because you enjoy keeping a fresh and tidy house. This could be your foray into cleaning homes for part time income. You get the idea! There are all kinds of ways to bring the wheel to ten...you just have to be willing to be creative, step out of your comfort zone, and make things happen.

Your Wheel of Life

DATE: _____

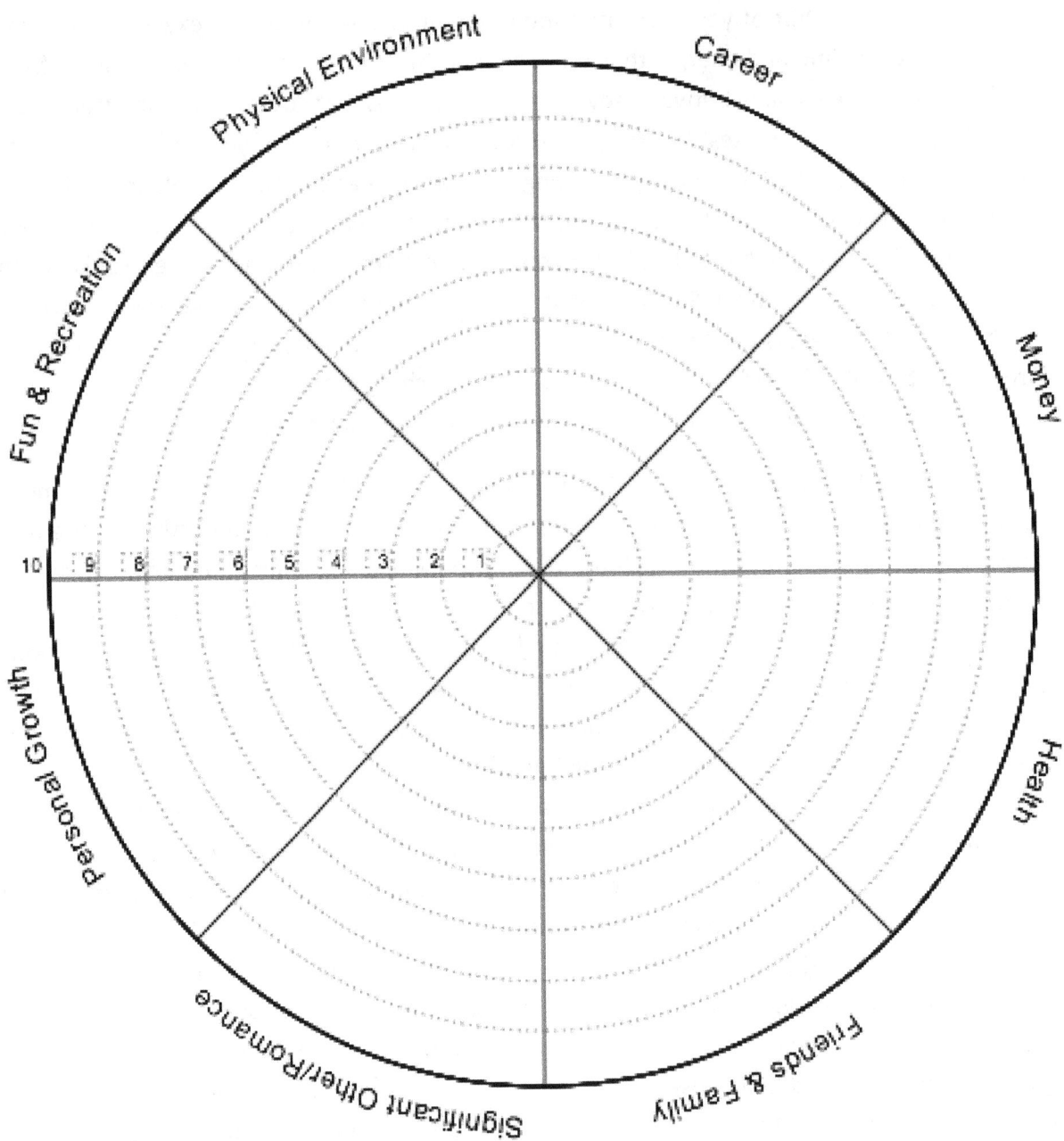

Step 1: The Value of Vision

The Vision you have for your ideal life is similar to when kids are asked what they want to be when they grow up. One child may want to be a Scientist, then another a Doctor, then a Teacher, Actor, Sports Star, Lawyer, and so on. If the person listening was a caring individual, they probably told you to stay in school, work hard, listen to your parents, and you can be anything you wanted. Developing your vision is no different. You can always pretend that you are five years old again, and dream your biggest dreams like it's no one's business but your own. #unfiltered

A note of caution...there will be people in your circle that will critique and ridicule your vision. There is a difference between a friend and a "frienemy." Some friends mean well when they give advice or guidance, and you should listen to them, as they sometimes are the voice of reason. On the other hand, it's your vision, and only you know whether it will manifest or not. Frenemies look like they mean well, but are plotting and/or counting on your downfall every moment. You should always pay close attention to conversations between you and them when you reveal your plans. Are they genuinely supportive, or mildly resenting your ambition? React accordingly.

Activity #1: Draw your Vision.

One of the greatest things you can do to build your vision is not only creating a vision board and tape, but actually drawing a snapshot of your vision. Now we aren't talking about a Picasso, it can be just a sketch of what you see. This page was left blank for you to draw what you see. Here's a start...draw what you would see in the first thirty minutes of waking in the morning. What would you wake up to?

Question #1: So what does your Vision look like?

- What kind of house would you like to have?

- What kinds of cars would you like to have?

- Describe your family life.

- Describe your perfect vacation.

- What charities would you contribute to? What charities would you join?

- How fit would you be?

- What would your bank account look like?

- Where would you work? Would you even work?

Activity #2: Read, Read, READ!

Find another book that interests you and READ IT! There aren't many things that are more inspiring than reading about places that you would like to travel to, houses you would like to live in, cars you would like to drive, events you would like to attend, family bonds you'd like to have, and the like. Sometimes, your first exposure to a different lifestyle is through reading about it, whether it be from a book, magazine, blog post, or any other literary medium. If the writer is good, you immerse yourself in the writing, and you can begin to see yourself with a life that encompasses all that you are reading about. So, if you aren't an avid reader, you should be...start quickly and then check out Activity #3. Although if you are a reader, DON'T EVER STOP! The most successful people in the world have voracious appetites for books, some digesting a book a month, while others digest a book a day.

Use the space below to research books on Amazon, and identify briefly why you think they would be great books to read or even additions to your library. Might I recommend a few?

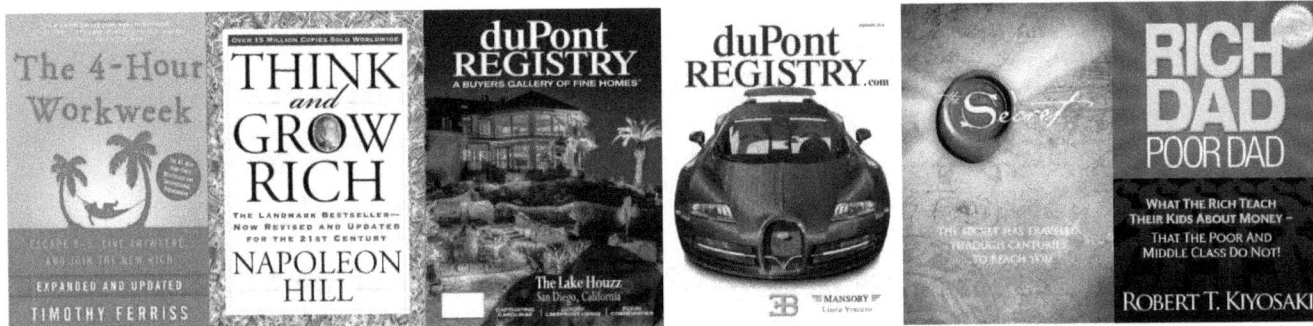

Question #2: What was the last good dream that you remember? Describe it to us.

Maybe one day we'll find the place
where our dreams and reality collide.

Activity #3: Watch and/or Listen to a Subliminal Program

Subliminal Programs are short media clips about ten minutes or less that combine multiple mediums to stimulate your mind and senses, programming your subconscious to carry out the messages you have been given. The clips I'm speaking of utilize images of wealth or success, auditory and visual messages of inspiration, and are rounded out by classical music or binaural beats that resonate at various frequencies to stimulate the mind. It may look and sound weird at first, but it's supposed to...it's a foreign action! It does work though, and it only does so if you use it consistently and regularly. Think about it...there are many cases where people have been brainwashed to commit heinous crimes during war, and anything you expose yourself to for extended periods of time becomes part of you due to programming. Why not use the science and practice for good to make yourself a success? Try it out...it can't hurt, right? Go to Youtube.com and type in the keyword string such as "meditation" "success" "binaural" and you will receive a host of videos that will help you meditate. I also have a version to try on my site at www.goodlife-coaching.com/tools, or you can try this one that is more audio than video. https://www.youtube.com/watch?v=5UeJUbdiY-w

Question #3: What routines have you developed that "book end" your days, allowing you to dream better dreams? Describe them, and if you haven't created any, what could you do to begin the practice?

This page was left blank for a reason. Use it to answer the Powerful Questions from this chapter in The M.A.P.

_____

_____

_____

_____

_____

_____

_____

_____

_____

_____

_____

_____

_____

_____

_____

_____

_____

_____

_____

Step 2: "Ginormous" Goals

If your Vision is your destination, then your goals are the locations on your M.A.P. that have to be reached. No excuses, no exceptions. In the book, I kept referring to one's goals as B.H.A.Gs and that they had to be S.M.A.R.T. If the acronyms are blowing your mind, pick up the book so you can decipher them.

The biggest reason goals are never met is what I call the "Reverse Incubation Period" or R.I.P. (COIN!) Most of the time, when you think of incubation it's in reference to something good, like an idea is baking...being created. The thought could be tossed around by a few people in a think tank or mastermind group. After it has passed through the minds of multiple people or deep thought by the individual, it then turns into a possible winner. Well, this isn't that. What I'm speaking of is a moment just after a person makes a decision toward a goal where they either move on it immediately, or continue to mull it over in their mind, or "R.I.P." it. What happens is the opposite of incubation...they made the decision without thinking about it, and now that they've decided on it, they think themselves out of the goal and it literally dies. Incubate your goals...don't R.I.P. 'em!

Question #1: What is a goal that you have accomplished in the past year? How did you accomplish it?

Activity #1: Create your list of S.M.A.R.T. B.H.A.Gs.

Try to make a list of five or more. Remember, they should look something like this...

- I will contribute 75 dollars to my savings every pay period, and by the end of this year, I will have saved over 50% of the cost for a one week, summer vacation in Hawaii, including airfare and amenities. #BOOM!

If remembering what S.M.A.R.T. means has you bogged down, then use the shortcut that you've known for years now...The Five W's, Who...What...When...Where...Why. If your goal can at least answer those five questions, you've created a pretty good one. *(COIN!)*

Activity #2: Create Your Race/Playing Field

If you haven't figured it out yet, having your visions and goals in front of you at all times are paramount to your success. One great way to illustrate your goals is to creatively remind yourself that they exist. What do I mean? I'm talking about taking a piece of poster board or science fair presentation board and making your goals visual, just like your vision. Remember though, your vision is the destination; it doesn't show you how to get there. That is your goals' job, and you should have milestones to keep you motivated along the way. Mine is a Football field, where I start in my territory and finish in the enemy's where the end zone is located. I have multiple routes on my field, so I can incorporate multiple goals. But they all end at the end zone. It has become a great visual that can be reused over and over by using Post-It notes. Be creative and have fun with this. Make a battle field where you have to get into enemy territory or a baseball field where you have to make it around the diamond. Once you're done, place it somewhere you will see it and modify it regularly. Place your post it note milestones all over it, and snatch 'em down when you've met that measure. I picked this template up at Etsy.com at https://www.etsy.com/listing/228118905/football-field-print-boys-room-nursery?ref=market and slapped it in a poster frame after printing it in on a poster maker. But that's just me, smarter not harder!

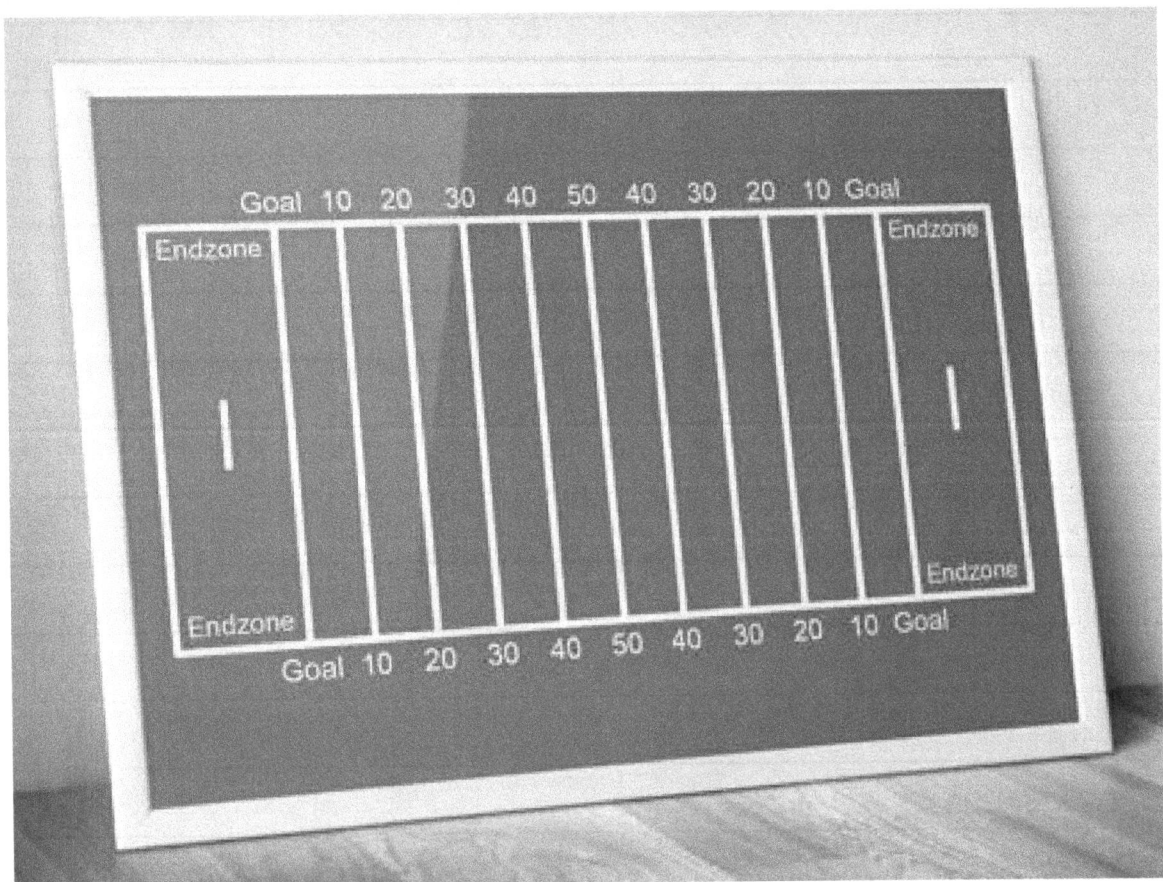

Activity #3: Post-It...Literally!

Again, getting your goals in front of you visually is just awesome, and the more places you can place them, the better. Which is why you should do just that, Post-It! Get a pad of post it notes and write a goal on each one. Do this about five times. Once you have your goals written, place those Post-Its in locations that you spend a lot of time, so you constantly remind yourself of your ambitions, and never have a thought that could be counterproductive to achieving your goals. Place them on the mirrors in your bedroom and bathroom, on your refrigerator, on the front of your TV screen (Prevention *COIN!*), in your car on the dashboard or steering wheel, on your desk at work, and if you can, go digital with them as well by creating a picture out of your list, then posting it as your computer and smartphone backgrounds and screensavers. It may sound like overkill, but is it really? How bad do you want to achieve everything you want?

Hey...it's another blank page!
I guess I should use it to answer some more Powerful Questions from this chapter, huh?

_____

_____

_____

_____

_____

_____

_____

_____

_____

_____

_____

_____

_____

_____

_____

_____

_____

_____

Step 3: Stabilize with Self-Discipline

Let's get right to the point...nothing, and I mean NOTHING, gets done by being lazy and undisciplined. To achieve your dreams, you're going to have to WORK...HARD! It is no walk in the park, and no one is going to hold your hand and make sure you have all of your I's dotted and T's crossed. People may guide or mentor you, but no one is going to make you do the work...that's your job! Being real, three-fourths of the stuff you're going to have to do, you're not going to want to do, even if it's going to catapult you to another level.

For example, I didn't think I was going to have to write this workbook for the masses, until after speaking with and listening to readers. I thought this journey was done! I didn't feel like I had to write it, but the people wanted it, so here it is. I spend my evenings into the mornings working on business after my wife and son have gone to bed, so I don't take away from my time being dad and husband. One of my former students (and now a close friend) spends his afternoons and weekends detailing vehicles. He doesn't necessarily like doing it, but it's a stepping stone to greater things, and it will provide him a cushion of comfort if and when calamity strikes...and it will! It always does! A big shout out to King Of Shine Detailing in North Carolina.

The HUSTLE & GRIND is SERIOUS! You have to have the discipline to say no to things, events, and even people that aren't part of your vision, don't see it, or aren't supportive of it. You have to have the discipline to get up early before everyone else rises and exercise if fitness is your goal, or put down the cigarettes if running a marathon is in your future. You have to look at this as if it were life or death, and that I'm going to die if I don't succeed.

One of the greatest things I can recommend is getting an Accountability Partner. (COIN!) Someone you can answer to that is where you want to be. It helps if it can be dual purpose, as in "you help me and I'll help you," but if it's not, no biggie. You just might end up having to pay them though for their time...and you should! Nothing in this world is free. You either pay with time, blood, sweat, tears, or actual money. They will be that person that will show up, regardless if you do or not. Since you committed to them and you don't want to lose face, you make an honest effort to be where they need you to be.

In the midst of writing this manual, I sought out the services of a personal trainer, because getting fit on my own hadn't worked at all, and I've been trying now for about four years. It just happens that this person also wanted to write a book. Well, I've banged out two (and a half if you count this workbook) and he's god-awfully fit, so we agreed to keep each other focused. I check in on him at least twice a week and once on the weekend to track his progress and help him overcome writer's block, and he meets me on the days he's not writing at the gym, or park, or wherever he has us working out at. We've been at it now for about two weeks. Neither of us has made great gains, but he's brainstorming and outlining his work and I'm starting to feel much better physically. We've got a great routine going, and that's what being disciplined is all about...consistency!

The other tip I'll complete this section with is the power of saying "No." Let's face it, we all want to be helpful to one person or another, but when you are constantly saying "Yes" to every person, project, and event under the blue sky, then you by default are saying no to something else. Also, it's hard to tell someone no. Just think about parents feeling the woes of telling their kids no sometimes. It burns them up! But here's the secret...if you create a "No Filter" for things that don't align with what your true vision and goals are, then you can start leaving yourself open to things that you would love to say yes to. (*COIN!*) What do I mean by this? Well, it's two-fold. There are places, events, and people that get in the habit of calling on the same individuals for everything, because they know subconsciously that said person will not say no. They may mean well, appreciate what you bring to the table, and you may come highly recommended, but deep down they know that they can count on you to say yes. Now, you may have had other plans, but since you were asked, you agreed to it. <u>Don't do it!</u> How else will they begin to build a broader basket of resources if you're always there to fill in? And believe it or not, if you say no, they will adjust and find someone else. So just say no. Be respectful about it, but kindly refuse. Your time is valuable, and you should be able to dictate who gets it and who will have to wait for another go round. The other side is this...the more you say no, the more time you have to say yes to projects and opportunities that can either launch you to greater heights, or really stir you soul.

I love coaching my son's youth soccer teams, and I've done it consistently in the fall, winter for Indoor Soccer, spring, and summer, for 3 years straight. We've got plenty of medals and trophies to show for it, so my reputation speaks for itself...I know and can coach Soccer. But this spring season was the first time I said no to being a sports coach. I heard there were disturbances in The Force when I declined. I did it because I wanted to regain some of my lost "me" time. I wanted to dedicate more time to building GOODLIFE!! Coaching and apparently I had to write this manual. I also wanted Mason to get experience playing under a different coach. He needed to be seen in the eyes of another coach, so they could expand on what's already been taught. The funny thing is that he decided not to even play this season...he wanted a break himself, believe it or not. So, that's what we did...we took a break from Soccer. It actually paid off in spades, because his schoolwork was getting more difficult, so we utilized some of that newfound extra time to beef up his Spelling, Reading, and Math skills. Also, because I said no, that left more time during the week and on weekends to build business, spend time with my son off the field, deepen my relationship with my wife, catch up with family, and just be. Try to say no more often. Your mind and spirit with thank you for it, but don't go overboard either! Sometimes, you can say no so much that people stop requesting you. Only if it doesn't align with your goals should you even consider saying no. There's nothing wrong with saying yes to some things, especially when they could be fun to do. You want people to "miss" your presence...not ignore you completely. One final point, and I've learned this the hard way...it's a lot easier to turn a "No" into a "Yes," than it is turning a "Yes" into a "No." (*COIN!*)

Question #1: What productive actions are you currently consistent with to the point where it's second nature or habit?

Activity #1: Scenario

Your supervisor has invited you to an informal gathering with some of the other executives from the company you work for. As their invited guest, it's a great honor and it shows the other execs that you are <u>the</u> one to watch on the fast track towards upper management. Your receive your e-vite in your work email, and see that it falls on the same day you promised your best friend a night out on the town for their birthday, which you've already canceled on once. How do you handle this situation? Explain your rationale.

OR

Activity #2: Scenario

You are a part-time, budding entrepreneur and have been working on plans for a prototype cellphone case. It's been submitted and pitched to multiple companies, and it shows promise. The time you have committed to the project while carrying a full time job and fulfilling your duties as a parent and spouse has worn you down. You feel if you don't get away for some R&R, you will probably meltdown. You plan a short weekend getaway for you and your spouse...they're looking forward to it as well. Just before booking the plans, you get a phone call from your agent stating a company wants to test the market with your prototype, and they need 500 renders of your case. There is no guarantee that you will make any revenue off of this deal, but to the victor goes the spoils. To accommodate this order, it will not only cost more than the getaway, but you'll have to dip into your savings. What do you do? Explain your reasoning.

OR

**Woohoo! Another blank page! Wait, don't tell me...
I should use it to answer some more Powerful Questions from
this chapter, right?**

Hey! Take a moment and check on your Wheel. Has anything improved since you've been attuned to it? Fill it in and let's see!

DATE: _____

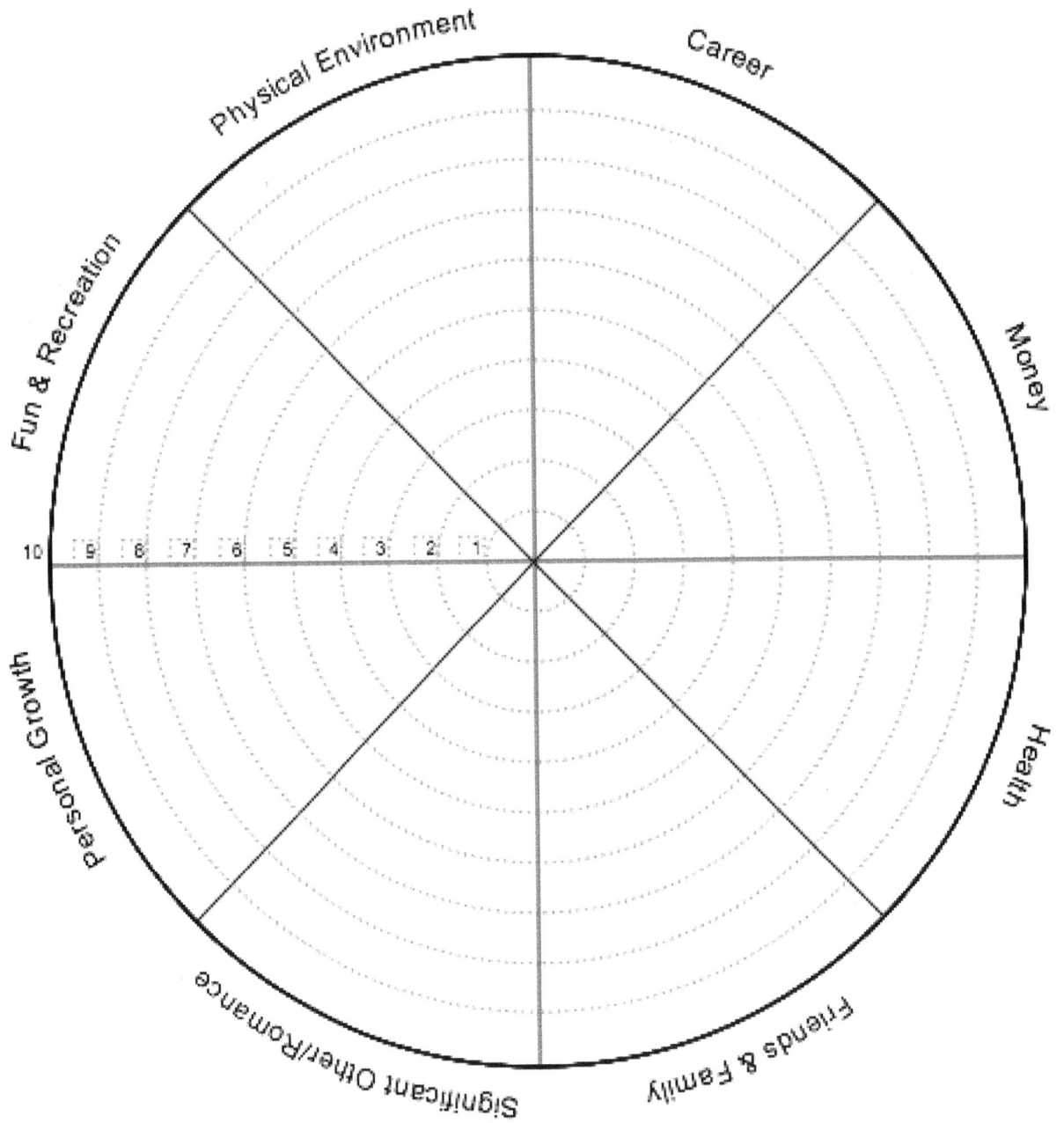

Step 4: Energize your Environment

You know what? The most rejuvenating action on the planet has got to be cleaning up one's personal space, at least in my opinion. I mean, geez...I feel better just cleaning and organizing my desk while writing this! There is nothing better than seeing a shine, inhaling the freshness, moving in the extra space, and realizing that your carpet really is tan and not muddy footprint brown! And it's fluid! Once you clean one part of your space, you want to clean the other parts of it, and then outside, and then your car, and then even yourself! It is sooo liberating! You know what that is right? That is the energy being released from your environment. You house, your yard, car, workspace, even your body, all have an energy about them, and when you allow them to breathe, revealing their true nature, their energy is passed on to you. Cool, right? In the book, I referenced your environment as simply being in your home, but it really is much more.

About your body...that too is part of your environment. It is such a permanent fixture, that you should take extreme care of it since you take it with you wherever you go. That is one part of the environment that you can never get away from, so why would you negatively weigh it down? Your body has energy in the form of fat, and if you have an excess of it, it is energy bound up...LET IT GO! MOVE MORE! When I was younger (read sans wife and kid) I used to think of my body as a temple. I called it "The Shrine," and nothing bad went into The Shrine. I used to stand in the mirror and "flex." I was never huge, overly muscular, or "veiny," but I looked good, felt good, and played at the top of my game. I'm far from that now, but I know I have to get back there, if even just to get back into some decent looking, cheaper, better quality clothing!

And, about the "green" and "blue" environments, you have to protect your little piece of it, and help others protect theirs as well. This planet, this Earth, is the only one we have right now. You have to preserve it so it survives not only for you to enjoy and thrive on, but for your legacy too. Have you ever seen a beautiful, green, pristine garden, only to have it marred by a piece of trash? It makes me want to get out of my car, go run up to the person's yard and pick it up, just because it hampered my viewing pleasure! If you see something that needs to be cleaned up, do it. Not only does it promote good citizenship in the community and stewardship of our Earth, but it gets you outdoors breathing fresh air, and you get that rush of energy from the Earth. Yes, the Earth has energy as well, and you can feel it. Think about the last time you went to the beach. You probably enjoyed yourself, right? Was it relaxing and therapeutic? Yes, those negative ions pulsating from the moving water interact with your body's chemistry and make you feel better. It's no wonder people flock to the coasts during the summer after a long, exhausting, and dark, fall and winter. Boost your energy levels by altering your surroundings.

Question #1: When was the last time you exercised to exhaustion? How did you feel afterwards?

TRAIN INSANE OR REMAIN THE SAME

Activity #1: Plan a healthy week for your diet with this chart.

Date: _____	Breakfast	Snack	Lunch	Snack	Dinner	Snack
Monday						
Tuesday						
Wednesday						
Thursday						
Friday						
Saturday						
Sunday						

- Are there any places that could be adjusted to better meet your goals?

Question #2: What actions can you put in place today to begin energizing your green and blue spaces?

Activity #2: Exercise!

Right now, drop down and give me...

- 10 push-ups
- 10 squats
- 20 crunches
- and Repeat 10 times, or until failure!

If you do this every morning/night for a month, I'm sure you will see something different in your upper body, lower body, midsection, and most of all, your attitude! Here is a calendar for you to monitor your progress. Make sure you fill it in!

Sunday	Monday	Tuesday	Wednesday	Thursday	Friday	Saturday

Damn Daniel! Back at it again with the blank white page! I know...I know...that was sooo spring 2016, but it was funny...sort of. Anyway, just answer the Powerful Questions from this chapter, 'mmkay?

_____

_____

_____

_____

_____

_____

_____

_____

_____

_____

_____

_____

_____

_____

_____

_____

_____

_____

Step 5: The Support Team

If you didn't know already, life is waaaay too short to have lackluster, negative, and simply dumb people that have no regard for your betterment surrounding you, especially the ones that have no goals, dreams, or drive themselves. I feel that I covered this pretty well in the book, so instead of reiterating what has been stated, I'll include some exercises and activities here to help facilitate the creation of your support team or further grow your inner circle while weeding out the naysayers.

Question #1: Social Media Support

Think about the tons of people you follow or that follow you on social media platforms like Facebook, Twitter, Instagram, Pinterest, YouTube, and Snapchat. Speaking primarily about those that you don't know, why did you choose to follow them? Why do you think they chose to follow you? Have you connected with any of your followers? What would you ask them/talk to them about if given the opportunity for a conversation? Would you feel weird if they reached out to you?

Activity #1: Lists of Five

This exercise illustrates the essential qualities that you'd expect to see in people that naturally will support you, the positive but non-essential qualities that are good to have but not important to you, and lastly the qualities that you don't want in your life at all. Once you are clear on what you want and don't want, you can more easily identify people that you would invite into your inner circle.

- Make a list of the top five qualities you look for in a person before you "invite" them into your inner circle.

_____   _____

_____   _____

_____

- Make a list of the top five qualities you avoid from people.

_____   _____

_____   _____

_____

- Make a list of the top five people of your inner circle. Write their names under each heading, and list their five best qualities, in your opinion.

Friend 1:	Friend 2:	Friend 3:	Friend 4:	Friend 5:

- How closely do their qualities matchup with what you look for in a person?

Activity #2: Create Your Own (Positive) Group

One of the greatest things about creating your own group is just that...it's yours...for now. A Group is an easy way to bring people together to interact with each other. It could be a means to relieve stress after a long day or week of work, or it could be a way to give back to the community. Better yet, it's a great way to meet new people and see how regular acquaintances engage with others, and it helps you brush up on your social skills. But it has to be something that is wanted or needed in your immediate environment. So, let's start the process.

1. Survey your area. What does the public need that you can provide in the form of a group? Are you an expert in that field, or do you know someone that is?

2. Gather details. What would they like to see? Ask to contact possible participants when they have more time to talk more in depth.

3. Begin to publicize what you want to do via social media, word of mouth, and even fliers. There is a simple template below. You may want to create this yourself, or hand this off to someone that will do it for you. Try not to spend any money on fliers outside of printing, but do make them eye catching.

   a. Name of Group: Make it Catchy!
   b. Session Title: Make It Catchy, too!
   c. Topic: What is this going to be about?
   d. Date: ???
   e. Time: When is the best time for you and people to participate? Get a consensus.
   f. Location: Should be at your house, a neutral location, or a friend's house that doesn't mind hosting your meeting. Public libraries, firehouses, churches,
   g. Guidelines: What rules/stipulations do you want to place in the group? Is it a social group...maybe everyone bring a snack item. Sponsored by: you may want to find a small business that wants some promotion, get them to pay for items at your gathering.

4. Promote, promote, promote to the date!

5. Have the group meeting.

6. Evaluate...how did it go? What went well and what flopped? Get some feedback from guests and then...Do It Again!

Activity #3: Join or Create a Mastermind Group.

Although you could place this activity under the previous one, I believe they are vastly different. A Positive Group could be seen as anything. A Music Appreciation Group could be seen as positive, just as a Board Game Group, but a Mastermind Group, no. Masterminds are groups of people (usually smart, highly energized, and ambitious or at least people with along the same professional level) that gather to discuss ideas, life strategies, topics of the day, business, and overall how to change the world.

Here is a short article on seven reasons why you should join one if ever invited to do so,

- http://www.forbes.com/sites/chicceo/2013/10/21/7-reasons-to-join-a-mastermind-group/#a80ec3b17ab7

and this article shows you the ins and outs of creating one.

- http://www.passionforbusiness.com/articles/mastermind-group.htm.

If you have the opportunity to be part of a mastermind, join! If they ask you to pay for membership, pay for it. If you can't, find a way! The amount of growth and mentorship you will experience is worth a lot more than the membership fee by far!

Blank page...Got it! Powerful Questions...Got 'em! Writing utensil...Got it! Filling in the white space...starting...NOW!

_____

_____

_____

_____

_____

_____

_____

_____

_____

_____

_____

_____

_____

_____

_____

_____

_____

_____

_____

_____

Step 6: Taking the Journey

Okay...this is it! You are on your way to creating the life you deserve! I am so proud of you for getting this far. But before you move on, just like in the book, I ask you...have you tried everything that has been asked of you? Are you prepared for success? If you aren't, please go back and finish what hasn't been done. Everything in this workbook was meant to help you and give personalized, handmade, success tools that you can utilize on your journey. No one jumps out of a plane without a parachute...neither should you!

If you need to...scroll back, otherwise, the open road awaits you!

Activity #1: Log Your Progress

A great way to identify if you are working toward your goals is to document the days you have actually attempted to do so. Use the lines below to log the dates, times, and mood you were in when you moved on your journey. You may see a pattern...most progress or the days you feel like moving forward are made when you are feeling happy, or frustrated. Keep that in mind.

Date	Time	Mood

It's a blank page...you know what to do. Handle it!

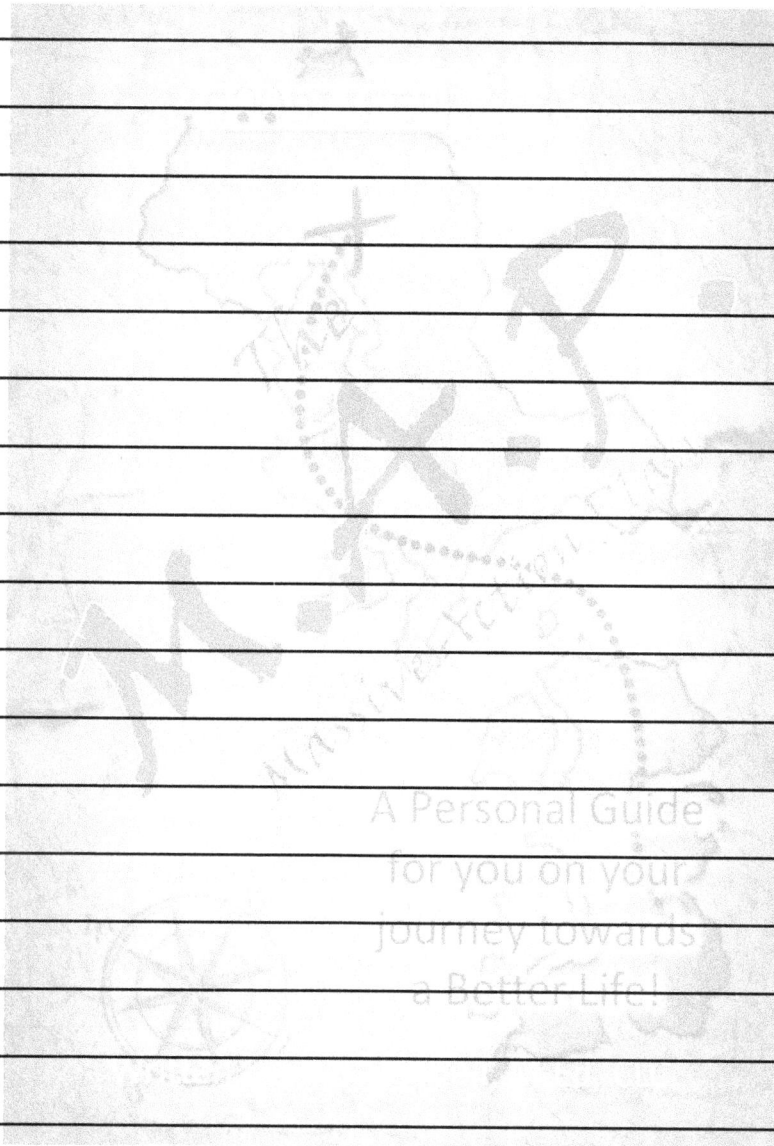

_____

_____

_____

_____

_____

_____

_____

_____

_____

_____

_____

_____

_____

_____

_____

_____

_____

_____

_____

Step 7: You Have Arrived!

WOOHOO!! Congrats! You made it! Your last activity is a simple one...GO FIND SOMEONE THAT WOULD BENEFIT FROM THIS JOURNEY!!

Activity #1: Make a List of Potential D.I.G.gers!

Brainstorm a list of everyone you know, young, middle aged, or old, whom may benefit from any of the teachings from The M.A.P. or this workbook. Then, tell each one of them about your transformation. But remember, you don't want to waste your efforts on those that aren't actively looking to get better. Only seek out those that want to grow now!

Share with them your journey through The M.A.P. and Let's D.I.G.

1. _____
2. _____
3. _____
4. _____
5. _____
6. _____
7. _____
8. _____
9. _____
10. _____
11. _____
12. _____
13. _____
14. _____
15. _____

16. _____
17. _____
18. _____
19. _____
20. _____
21. _____
22. _____
23. _____
24. _____
25. _____
26. _____
27. _____
28. _____
29. _____
30. _____

48

It's the LAST BLANK PAGE!
Fill it in with you know what from you know where!

_____

_____

_____

_____

_____

_____

_____

_____

_____

_____

_____

_____

_____

_____

_____

_____

_____

_____

_____

_____

_____

_____

Hey! Here's the last one! Take a look at your Wheel. You should be close to that coveted Golden Circle now! If not, keep pushing, but I know it looks good!

DATE: _____

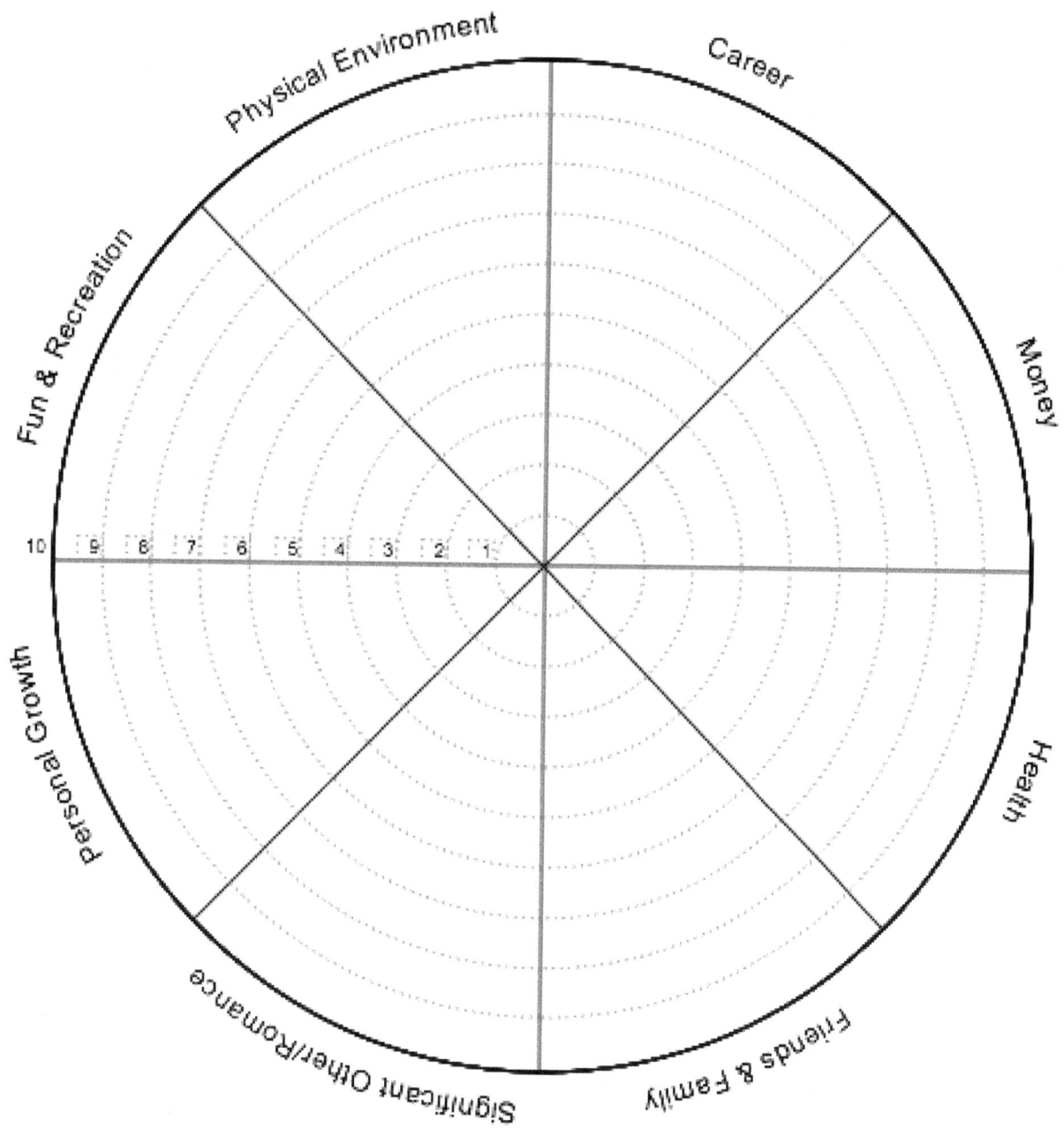

Conclusion:

This has been a labor of love, as in, I love doing what I do and I love you as well. You guys edify everything that I have worked so hard for, and your new success story is also mine. I thank you for taking the time to work through both The M.A.P. and Let's D.I.G. If at any given time you feel that you are "stuck in the mud" (reference from The M.A.P.), please go back through these books, find out where you're lacking or would like to improve, and regenerate the greatness inside of you. This manuscript was never meant to be an ending, but a beginning...and continuation, as we never really finish becoming who we really want to be until the day we leave this world. And when that day comes, I want you to be ready, with no regrets, having lived the life you deserved.

Take Care and God Bless!

Chester

About the Author & GOODLIFE!! Coaching

Chester is the Owner and Lead Coach of GOODLIFE!! Coaching. He has over fourteen years of experience in the Education field, eleven of those as a classroom teacher and the remainder serving as a Prevention & Intervention Specialist for Accomack County Public Schools. In this capacity, he focuses his efforts on Anti-Bullying, Character Education, encouraging positive student-teacher relationships, mentoring At-Risk Youth, Truancy Prevention, and Threat Assessment. He also is a member of the International Coaching Federation (ICF) and a member of the Black Life Coaches Network (BLC.net).

Chester is a 2001 graduate of Hampton University. He has obtained a Master's Degree in Education Administration from Salisbury University, and earned his Coaching Certification from Academic Life Coaching Inc. He is an avid reader of self-help/leadership books and a diehard gamer. He regularly volunteers his time with Youth Soccer as a Coach and serves as a Parent Leader for Cub Scout Pack 300 in Parksley, VA. He resides on Virginia's Eastern Shore with his wife Nyoka and son Mason.

You can contact Chester for motivational speaking, coaching, or book signing at 757-709-2832 and at chester.hall@goodlife-coaching.com.

GOODLIFE!! Coaching is a life coaching practice that helps individuals realize their vision and accomplish their goals. The company specializes in working with young adults and at-risk adolescents; although they are open to other clients as well. GOODLIFE!! Coaching has a subsidiary brand, BULLYPROOF!! Coaching, which helps elementary and middle school students build life empowerment skills while combating the effects of bullying.

Visit GOODLIFE!! Coaching online at www.goodlife-coaching.com. While there, subscribe to our monthly newsletter and blog, The BLOOPRINT!! You can follow us on Twitter and Periscope @AGOODLIFE, on Instagram @g00dlifecoaching, on Snapchat @chesterhall, and on Facebook at www.facebook.com/g00dlifecoaching. We love getting feedback about what we're doing and hearing about your life changing journeys!